HEAVEN AND MIRTH®

THE Prodigal Son

Oh, Brother!

AND
OTHER BIBLE STORIES TO TICKLE YOUR SOUL

by Mike Thaler

Illustrated by Dennis Adler

Faith KiDs™

*Equipping Kids
for Life*

Dedicated to
Laurel Lee Thaler,
who led me to the Lord.
With love,
Mike

THE PRODIGAL SON, OH, BROTHER
© 2000 by Mike Thaler for text and Dennis Adler for illustrations
FaithKids™ is a registered trademark of Cook Communications Ministries.

HEAVEN AND MIRTH® is a registered trademark of Mike Thaler

Published in association with the literary agency of Alive Communications, Inc.,
1465 Kelly Johnson Blvd., Suite 320, Colorado Springs, CO 80920.

Edited by Jeannie Harmon
Designed by Clyde Van Cleve

Cook Communications, Colorado Springs, Colorado 80918
Cook Communications, Paris, Ontario
Kingsway Communications, Eastbourne, England

First printing, 2000
Printed in Singapore
04 03 02 01 00   5 4 3 2 1

Thaler, Mike, 1936–
    The Prodigal Son, Oh Brother!: and other Bible stories to tickle your soul / by Mike Thaler;
        illustrated by Dennis Adler. p. cm. – (Heaven and mirth; 2)
    Summary: Five stories based on incidents taken from the New Testament and written in a humorous way.
    ISBN 0-7814-3263-4
    1. Bible stories, English 2. Forgiveness–Religious aspects-Christianity Juvenile literature.
    I. Adler, Dennis, (Dennis H), 1942– II. Title. III. Series: Thaler, Mike, 1936– Heaven and mirth; 2.
    BS551.2.T46 1999
    225.9'505–dc21
                                                                                            99-31548
                                                                                                CIP

Letter from the Author

Taking this opportunity, I would like to share with you how this book came about. Born sixty-two years ago, I have been a secular children's book author most of my life. I was also content to have a fast-food relationship with God from the drive-by window. At the age of sixty, I came into the banquet by inviting Jesus Christ into my heart. Since then my life has been a glorious feast. These stories are part of that celebration.

One night I sat and watched a sincere grandfather trying to read Bible stories to his squirming grandchildren. I asked him, "Aren't there any humorous retellings of Bible stories that are vivid and alive for kids?" He rolled his eyes and said, "This is it." The kids rolled their eyes, too.

This made me sad, for the Bible is the most exciting, valuable, and alive book I know—as is its Author. So I went into my room, with this in mind, and wrote "Noah's Rainbow."

Since then God has anointed me with sixty stories that fire my imagination and light up my heart.

They are stories which, I hope, are filled with the joy, love, and spirit of the Lord.

Mike Thaler
West Linn 1998

Nuggets from Goldie the miner prophet:
"It's Never Too Late to Eat Right."

Author's Note

I have conscientiously tried to follow each story in word and spirit as found in the Bible. But in some cases, for the sake of storytelling, I have taken minor liberties and added small details. I pray for your understanding in these instances.

3

The Prodigal Son
Oh, Brother!

AMAN HAD TWO SONS.
The older one, Goodhew,
was a responsible kid.
He always did his homework,
helped his dad with the dishes,
and fed his hamster.

The younger one, Peewee, was not.

He cheated on his tests, he left his room a mess,
and all his pets died of starvation.

Now when the boys got older,
Goodhew went into his dad's business.
But Peewee took half
of his dad's bank account,
and split for the big city.
There he squandered
his fortune on restaurants,
gambling, and taxicabs.
He soon was evicted
from his penthouse,
and lived in the doorway
of a pet store, where the owner
occasionally fed him polly seeds.

While at home, Goodhew
doubled his dad's business,
married a nice Jewish girl,
and gave his dad six grandkids
with straight teeth.

Many polly seeds later,
Peewee started to miss home!

"Even Goodhew's hamster
has it better than I do.
At least he has clean
wood chips to sleep on,
and a wheel to run in.
I'll go home, and see
if I can stay with the hamster."
So Peewee trudged back home.

When his dad spotted him
crawling down the road,
he ran out, lifted him up,
and hugged him.

"Father, I have sinned
against heaven and you.
I am no longer worthy
to be called your son—
just call me *Hamster.*"

"No, no, it's okay, Son,"
cheered the dad,
kissing the tears
from Peewee's eyes.
"Welcome home!"

Then his dad ran a hot bubble bath,
gave Peewee his best silk robe,
his Rolex watch,
his new Italian shoes,
and said, "Let's party, Son!"

When Goodhew came home
and heard the music,
he thought the party
was for him. But when he
walked in and saw the
"Welcome Home Peewee"
balloons, he grew very angry,
and stalked out.

His dad ran after him,
"Hey, Son, don't be a party pooper.
Peewee's home!"

"Forget it, Dad, I worked hard for you
all these years and you never gave me
balloons, not even on my birthday."

"But Peewee was lost
and now he's found."

"Well, let him get lost again!"
muttered Goodhew.

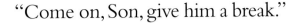

"Come on, Son, give him a break."

"I'd like to," snarled Goodhew.

Just then Peewee came out.
"Hey, Goodhew, how's it goin'?
I see by the hands of my new Rolex
that it's time to cut the cake."

"Why don't you just cut out,"
barked Goodhew.

"Now boys, cut it out.
Shake hands and I'll name
this whole place
after both of you."
So they did, and he did,
and that spot is still called
Two-son, Arizona.

THE END

Nuggets from Goldie, the miner prophet:
"When a lost lamb returns, you should flock to him."

For the real story, read Luke 15:11–32.

10

Peter in the Pokey
The Great Escape

KING HAIR-ROD JR. WAS NOT A GOOD RULER.
In fact, he was many inches short of being one.
He also wasn't into religious freedom.
He started arresting Christians,
and even put James to death.
When his approval rating went up,
he arrested Peter.

It was Passover and Hair-Rod Jr.
didn't want to spoil
the holiday spirit,
so he chained Peter in jail
with sixteen guards around him,
and planned to try him later.

When the church heard this, first they thought
they'd have a bake sale of escape cakes
with files inside. Then they thought
they'd run a bingo night to raise bail.
But instead they decided
to sit down and ask God
for Peter's deliverance.

So they prayed, and they prayed,
and the night before the trial,
their prayers were answered.
An angel appeared in Peter's cell and
woke him up. It wasn't even visiting
hours. Peter rubbed his eyes.
"Are you my lawyer?" he said.

"Quick, get up!" said the angel, nudging him.

Peter stood up and his chains fell off.
"Wow!" said Peter. "Are you Houdini?"

"Get dressed," said the angel,
nudging him again. "We're getting out of here."

So Peter got dressed and followed the angel,
for he thought it was all a dream.
They walked past the first guards,
then past the second guards.

"This is cool," said Peter. "I hope
I don't wake up until we're back home."

The main gate opened wide
before them, and Peter walked out.

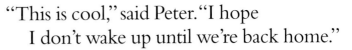

"This is the best dream
I've ever had," said Peter.

The angel pinched him.
"This ain't no dream, kid!"

When Peter looked around,
he was free, and the angel was gone.
He ran to Mary's house
and knocked on the door.
There were many Christians inside
praying for his release.

"Get the door, Rhoda," they said.
So Rhoda looked out the window and saw Peter.

"Well, who is it, Rhoda?" everyone asked.

"It's Peter!"

"Oh, yeah," they scoffed, "it's probably just a Passover
trick-or-treater."

"No, it's Peter!" she asserted.

"Oh, yeah, it's probably just someone selling Girl Scout cookies."

"It's Peter!" she insisted.

The knocking continued
so they all went to the door
and opened it.
And lo and behold
there stood Peter.

"What took ya so long?"
he said.
"My hand is killing me."

"We thought
you were in prison,"
they said.

"Shhhh," said Peter,
and he told them
how the Lord
had given him a big break.

"Wow!" they all said.
"Let's have a CELL–EBRATION!"

In the morning, there was quite a commotion
when all the guards found Peter missing.

"You had him last," they said to one another.

They all bumped into each other
searching the whole prison.
They looked in the lost-and-found
and the gift shop, but they couldn't
find hide nor hair of Peter—
and he had a lotta hair.

When Hair-Rod Jr. heard the news,
he was not happy.
In spite of union pleas,
he had all the guards put to death.
Then he put in thicker bars
and changed all the locks.
He would have changed the bagels too,
but during a public address,
an angel of the Lord struck him down with a sword,
and he was immediately eaten by worms.

THE END

Nuggets from Goldie, the miner prophet:
"Bars do not a prison make, when God is planning the escape!"

For the real story, read Acts 12.

A Rich Young Man
Investing in Heaven

ONE DAY A RICH YOUNG MAN drove up to Jesus and His disciples in a new *Ferrari*.

"Nice car," said Bartholomew.

"Nothing compared to God's chariot," said Jesus.

"Good Teacher," said the young man, "what do I have to do to get into heaven?"

"Well, first of all, no one is really good—except God."

"I can live with that," said the young man.

"Second, you must follow all of God's commandments."

"I can live with that, too," he nodded.

"And thirdly, you must sell everything you have and give the money to the poor."

The young man was quiet.
He thought, then he spoke.
"You mean sell my car,
my city house and my desert
house, my polo pony, my gold
cigarette lighter,
and all my credit cards?"

"You got it," said Jesus.

"Do you have a brochure?"

"No," smiled Jesus.

"I'll get back to you,"
said the young man.
"I have to check with my

investment broker and my girlfriend." And he got into his car and zoomed away.

"Ya know," sighed Jesus, "it's as easy for a rich man to enter heaven as it is for a camel to go through the eye of a needle."

"Yeah, but I bet he went from zero to sixty in eight seconds," said Bartholomew.

"Going nowhere fast is not a blessing," smiled Jesus. "And by the way, Bartholomew, I think you should cancel your subscription to *Road and Track*."

THE END

Nuggets from Goldie, the miner prophet:
"If all you want is profit, you'll never be a prophet."

For the real story, read Luke 18:18-29.

The Conversion of Saul
The Bounty Hunter Finds the Bounty

S AUL WAS FAMOUS
for killing Christians.
Christians shook in their sandals
at the mere mention of his name.

"Saul."

SHAKE, SHAKE, SHAKE.

He left no stoning unturned to find one.

He loved to watch them rock and roll.
So everyone was surprised
when God chose Saul to deliver
His Word to the Gentiles.

It happened on the road to Damascus.
Suddenly a light from heaven
flashed around Saul.
He fell to the ground
and God spoke to him.

**"Hey, Saul, what's with you?
Why do you pick on Me?"**

"Who are You, Lord?"

"Who do you think I am? I'm Jesus. Now get up and go to Damascus for further instructions."

Saul got up, but when he opened his eyes, he was blind. So his friends led him into town.

Then the Lord called on Ananias.

"Ananias."

"Yes, Lord."

"Go to the house of Judas on Straight Street, and ask for a blind man named Saul."

"You want me to go
to the house of Saul,
in a blind alley, and ask for Judas?"

"No, no. Get it straight!"

"Oh, go to the house of Judas,
and ask for Saul. I got it.
But Lord, Saul is not supposed
to be user-friendly."

**"Go! I have chosen him
to deliver My Word
to the Gentiles."**

STRAIGHT ST.

"Okay, if You say so, Lord."

So Ananias went to Saul
   with much trepidation,
      and put his hands over Saul's eyes.

"The Lord Jesus Christ
   has sent me
      to restore your sight,
         and to show you the way."

Immediately Saul opened
   his seeing eyes and was filled
   with the Holy Spirit.

"I was blind, but now I see,"
   cried Saul.

"That's not a bad line,"
   said Ananias, who also did
      a little songwriting
         on the side.

So Saul changed his name
to Paul, and went out
and started preaching
the Gospel in a mighty
powerful way.

Everyone was surprised,
considering his past record,
and he brought many to the Lord.
He became a traveling *salesman*
for God, instead of a traveling
assailant of God.

THE END

Nuggets from Goldie, the miner prophet:
"You are much richer when you have a change of heart."

For the real story, read Acts 9:1–22.

Paul and Eutychus
Bored to Death

PAUL WAS A PREACHER. Now preachers love to talk about God. They can talk for hours. They can talk for days. They can even talk for weeks. When Paul was in Troas, he decided to give a little after-dinner sermon.

Around midnight,
a young man named Eutychus
fell asleep. Unfortunately,
he was sitting by an open window.
Unfortunately,
he fell out of the window.
Unfortunately,
the window
was on the second floor.
Unfortunately,
he died.

Paul stopped talking.
He rushed downstairs
and fell upon Eutychus.
Luckily Paul had C.P.R. training
(Christ Power Revival)
and he gave Eutychus
heart-to-heart resuscitation.

Eutychus opened his eyes and blinked.
"Is the sermon over?" he asked.

"Not yet," said Paul, and they carried
the young man back upstairs,
and sat him down in the corner.

Paul went on talking till he had to leave
the next morning. The people
were greatly relieved.

Now pastors today
have learned a lot from this story.
Firstly, they put their churches
on the first floor.
And secondly,
they put all the windows
up high,
so when their
parishioners fall asleep,
they won't fall out.

THE END

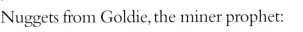

Nuggets from Goldie, the miner prophet:
"In order for your soul to awake, your body has to be up, too!"

For the real story, read Acts 20:7–12.

HEAVEN AND MIRTH®

THE Prodigal Son
Oh, Brother!

Age: 6 and up
Life Issue: Understanding God's forgiveness so that your child can forgive others.
Spiritual Building Block: Forgiveness

Learning Styles

Help your child learn about forgiveness in the following ways:

Sight: Watch a video version of the Prodigal Son, the Rich Young Ruler, or Paul's conversion. What was the attitude of the main characters in each story? When confronted with their choices, how did they change? How should we act when we realize that we have done wrong?

Sound: Discuss with your child the difference between when someone uses angry words and someone asks to be forgiven. What do the two examples sound like? Why is it important to ask for forgiveness of those we hurt? How do you feel when you ask someone to forgive you? How do you feel when they say, "I forgive you?"

Touch: Tape a sheet of paper with the word "GOD" written on it to one wall in a room. Have family members stand with their backs to the wall and close to each other. Tell them that when we are close to God, we behave in ways that please Him more. Have each person name actions that don't please God. With each action, have that person take a step away from the wall and away from other family members. Explain how bad choices require that we confess our sin and ask God to forgive us. Then we can move close to Him again.

Adapted from *Basic Christian Beliefs* by Jim Weidmann and Kurt Bruner,
published by Chariot Victor Publishing, page 58-59.